Blyton

Pocket **BIOGRAPHIES**

Series Editor C.S. Nicholls

Highly readable brief lives of those who have played a significant part in history, and whose contributions still influence contemporary culture.

Enid Blyton

GEORGE GREENFIELD

SUTTON PUBLISHING

First published in 1998 by
Sutton Publishing Limited · Phoenix Mill
Thrupp · Stroud · Gloucestershire · GL5 2BU

British Library Cataloguing in Publication Data

A catalogue record for this book is available from the British
Library

ISBN 0-7509-1633-8

ALAN SUTTON™ and SUTTON™ are the
trade marks of Sutton Publishing Limited

Typeset in 13/18 pt Perpetua.
Typesetting and origination by
Sutton Publishing Limited.
Printed in Great Britain by
The Guernsey Press Company Limited,
Guernsey, Channel Islands.

To Georgie and Miles,

who enjoyed the first ever

Noddy in Toyland *pantomime*

CONTENTS

LIST OF ILLUSTRATIONS

1. Enid Blyton in her twenties.
2. Enid Blyton in the library at her home, Green Hedges, 1945.
3. Enid in the garden at Green Hedges with her second husband, Kenneth Darrell Waters.
4. A book launch at Hatchards, 1952.
5. Noddy and Big Ears taking a drive in Toyland.
6. Enid Blyton surrounded by Noddy merchandise.
7. The cover of *Last Term at Malory Towers*, published in 1951.
8. Enid relaxing at home with her Siamese cat.
9. Enid at work.
10. Enid's eldest daughter Gillian Baverstock with Norman Wright, 1994.
11. The cover of Enid Blyton's *The Sea of Adventure*, published in 1948.

Illustration no. 4 is the property of the author. Mr Norman Wright is the copyright holder of no. 10. The remaining illustrations have been reproduced by kind permission of Enid Blyton Limited.

ACKNOWLEDGEMENTS

My warm thanks are due to Gillian Baverstock and Imogen Smallwood, Enid Blyton's daughters, Ida Pollock and her daughter Rosemary, Eva Rice, author of *Who's Who in Enid Blyton*, Tony Summerfield and Norman Wright of the Enid Blyton Literary Society, David Lane and Victoria Marks of the Enid Blyton Company and Christine Nicholls, my ever helpful editor. I am much indebted to Alison Flowers, the in-house editor, with her unerring eye for misprints and mistakes.

Well as I thought I knew Enid Blyton, I discovered several new facts from reading Barbara Stoney's standard biography and am correspondingly grateful to her.

CHRONOLOGY

1897   **11 August**. Enid Blyton born, the first child of Thomas Carey Blyton and his wife Theresa (née Harrison)

1907   Enrols at St Christopher's School for Girls, Beckenham, Kent

1910   Her father leaves home to live with another woman

1915   Leaves St Christopher's as head girl

1916   Attends the Guildhall School of Music

1916   Attends the National Froebel Union course, Ipswich

1917   *Nash's Magazine* accept her first three poems

1918   **December**. Completes her Froebel course with first-class passes and one distinction

1919   **January**. Begins teaching at Bickley Park School

1920   **January**. Becomes nursery governess to four children in Surbiton

1922   *Teachers' World* publish several of her poems and short stories

1922   Her first book is published – *Child Whispers*, a short collection of poems

1923   Meets Hugh Pollock, editor at George Newnes, publishers. Earns more than £300 from her writing

1924	**August**. Marries Hugh Pollock at Bromley Registry Office
1925	Annual earnings reach £1,200 (about £50,000 in current terms)
1926	Begins to edit *Sunny Stories*
1929	Moves to Old Thatch, Bourne End, with Hugh
1930	Travels to Madeira on a cruise
1931	**July**. Gives birth to Gillian
1935	**October**. Second daughter, Imogen, born
1938	Moves to Green Hedges
1941	Meets Kenneth Darrell Waters, a surgeon
1942	First Famous Five book published
1942	**December**. Divorces Hugh
1943	**October**. Marries Kenneth Darrell Waters
1949	*Little Noddy Goes To Toyland* published
1950	Copyright holding company formed – Darrell Waters Limited
1954	**Christmas**. *Noddy in Toyland* pantomime produced
1955	*The Famous Five* play produced. Noddy puppet films on ITV
1961	First signs of Alzheimer's disease
1967	**September**. Kenneth dies
1968	**28 November**. Enid Blyton dies

PREFACE

Fifty years ago, as a young publisher, I wrote out of the blue to Enid Blyton wondering if my firm could reprint some of her titles. She replied at once, asking pertinent questions about the company and myself before agreeing to a contract.

Over the next few years, a business friendship developed. On leaving publishing to become a literary agent, I wrote to my authors wishing them well. A few days later, Enid telephoned to ask if I would represent her, as she had not previously had a proper agent. My surprised but delighted acceptance was immediate.

Until her death almost sixteen years later, I had the privilege of a ringside seat in all her varied enterprises, some of which I saw develop from their beginnings. Thus, in writing this short biography, I have found it impossible to adopt an arm's length approach, but have tried only to bring myself in at important points where I was personally involved.

CHILD, WOMAN, AUTHOR, WIFE

Enid Mary Blyton, the eldest of three children, was born on 11 August 1897 at Lordship Lane, East Dulwich, London. Her father, Thomas Carey Blyton, came from a rural family which had become involved in the wool trade, but he grew up in Sheffield and had become a cutlery salesman. At the age of twenty-six, he married a Miss Harrison from his home town. Shortly afterwards, they moved to the London suburbs when he was promoted to represent his firm in the City. Enid was born in the small flat above a shop in East Dulwich. A few months later, the family moved to a house in nearby Beckenham and, after another brief period, to a larger one in the neighbouring Clockhouse Road.

Thomas Blyton had improved his prospects by changing from cutlery sales to a better job at a clothes warehouse — hence the family moved to more spacious houses. But he was no intellectual philistine. It was the age of Samuel Smiles, of self-improvement through reading and studying at home. He was interested in astronomy, learned to play the piano, taught himself foreign languages and read voraciously. Two years after Enid was born, his wife, Theresa, gave birth to a boy, Hanly, and another son, Carey, three years after that. But Enid, it seems, grew up to be his favourite. She took after him in looks and from an early age showed the same wide interest in the arts and in nature. Under his tuition, she learned to grow flowers from seed and was as thrilled as he was when they came up in all their varieties. He taught her to play the piano when she was six and made her practise every day. Like him, but within her own age-group, she was a promiscuous reader. The one weakness that emerged when she went to nursery school was her failure to grasp simple arithmetic.

When she was ten, she entered a local school, St Christopher's School for Girls. It was then and for the next few years that she became a bone of contention between her father and mother, whose marriage was already under considerable strain.

Theresa believed strongly in the prevailing motto that a woman's place was in the home. Women were to be domesticated, grow up, marry and have children; that was their sanctioned role. Enid should stop this 'mooning around' with her nose in a book all the time. She should help out with the housework and the cooking (the family had moved to the even larger house in Clockhouse Road by this time). Thomas naturally defended his daughter, of whose growing accomplishments he was enormously proud.

But, when Enid was reaching puberty, a worse domestic conflict broke out. In spite of his abiding affection for his daughter, Thomas had fallen out of love with his wife and was conducting what seems to have been a passionate affair with another woman. In the Edwardian era, divorced women of the middle classes were held to be pariahs and Theresa did not see why she, the 'innocent party', should become a social outcast. She refused Thomas a divorce. In 1910, he left the family home and at his expense they shortly moved to a larger detached house in a nearby quiet road. He set up his own business in London and continued to support his family and pay for his children's education.

We can imagine the subterfuges and excuses that the single mother and her growing family had to resort to in order to explain away the father's permanent absence. Tongues must have wagged in suburban Beckenham and rumours abounded. If that was not enough stress to place on Enid, Thomas's departure must have been a great emotional shock for her. Rejection – for that was how it must have appeared to the girl entering her teens – by the father she loved devotedly, who understood her, who encouraged her in the arts and praised the results of her efforts, in favour of a strange woman was a grievous blow. But in those prim, lace-curtain days, keeping up appearances was all-important. According to Barbara Stoney, whose detailed biography *Enid Blyton* is a valuable source, Enid maintained an air of normality at her private school, when she must have been seething with anger and grief. When, eighteen years later and married to her first husband Hugh, she found it difficult to conceive, the gynaecologist she consulted told her that she had a much under-developed uterus, equivalent to that of a young girl aged twelve or thirteen. Psychologists might claim that a series of deep emotional shocks at about that age had prevented her from achieving sexual maturity.

Outwardly, at St Christopher's School, she showed no signs of any inward stress. She was strong and athletic and good at games, excelling in lawn tennis and lacrosse. She was an ardent classroom pupil and won several prizes for her work, notably English composition. She even ran a small magazine privately among her friends, to which she contributed short stories.

The First World War seems to have had little or no impact on her. Thomas Blyton would have been in his mid-forties in 1914, too old for conscription. Enid's two younger brothers were well below the age for call-up. Beckenham was then a pleasantly wooded suburb, away from the mainline railway stations and ports where tens of thousands of troops embarked – and far fewer returned. Somehow, one might have expected the poetry of Rupert Brooke and Wilfred Owen to appeal to this widely read girl, but there is no evidence that it did. This is strange, because Enid herself had been encouraged by the famous Arthur Mee, in one of whose papers she had a poem published when she was fourteen, to continue writing verses. Also during the war, in

March 1917, she actually had a poem accepted by *Nash's Magazine*.

The friction between Enid and her mother continued to grow. Theresa, set in her ways, still maintained that a woman's place was in the home. A career was to be discouraged. The younger woman rebelled and refused to accept the narrow role her mother planned for her. Already, in her late teens, she knew she was destined for a more exciting future. She could tell stories that held her younger listeners spellbound, she could instruct, and she could be an example. The apex was reached with her appointment as head girl of the school.

Popular as she was as an oral storyteller, initially she had little success when she came to put the words on to paper. She told me, her agent, more than once in her later years that she had papered the walls of her room with rejection slips from magazines and newspapers. As with many 'romancers', Enid could exaggerate at times to achieve artistic effect, but there is no doubt that she was widely snubbed at first. It was her determination and driving ability, coupled with the encouragement of her best friend, Mabel Attenborough, that kept her writing.

Her Aunt May was a professional pianist and her father, who had taught himself to become proficient at the piano, hoped and expected that his daughter would follow suit. From an early age, Enid had shown great determination in whatever she undertook. She practised for hours, took the various piano examinations (including LRAM) and, on leaving St Christopher's, even enrolled at a school for musicians, the Guildhall School of Music and Drama. Gradually, she realized that her heart was not in it – but she had no alternative at that time. Her scripts were being returned, accompanied by rejection slips, in almost every post. She could not simply hang around at home, driven by her increasingly antagonistic mother to spend her daylight hours on domestic chores. As pets were not tolerated by the house-proud elder woman, Enid did not have the benefit of that emotional safety valve.

In 1916, on holiday in Suffolk, Enid met Ida Hunt, who taught the kindergarten at Ipswich High School. Miss Hunt had been trained in the Froebel method and she also taught at a local Sunday school. She invited Enid along to help her and quickly learned that this girl, who was still in her teens, had an innate talent for communicating. When she told them Bible stories, the children responded at once and displayed an absorbed interest, which the editors whom she was continuing to bombard with material signally lacked. The truth dawned on her — she must make a career as a teacher.

In *Enid Blyton*, Barbara Stoney tells the interesting story of how Thomas arranged for a phrenologist to feel Enid's 'bumps' when she was about eight in order to forecast the future. He was apparently hoping to hear that she had a great musical career ahead, but the eventual report read: 'This child will turn to teaching when she develops. It is, and will be, her great gift.'

Enid was still legally a minor and her father, although long separated from her mother, was still officially her legal guardian. Although he was greatly disappointed when she sought his permission to take up a career in teaching, she was so positive that it was the right choice, and he felt such affection for her, that he almost readily gave his permission. Ipswich High School employed trainee teachers who learned as they taught. The Froebel method was used at the kindergarten level. In spite of the unremitting pressure of teaching in the daytime and studying for her examinations after work, Enid still found time to compose verses. Ironically, the rejection slips now changed to acceptances – at least, occasionally. As mentioned, in 1917 *Nash's Magazine* accepted a sentimental poem entitled 'Have You . . .?', the first-recorded publication of an Enid Blyton work. She was in her twentieth year.

By the end of 1918, Enid was a qualified Froebel teacher, having achieved first-class examination passes in most subjects (but only a 'second' in literature). The head mistress gave her an imposing reference and the following month she became a junior teacher at Bickley Park School, a mile or two from the area where she had grown up. The children took to her and she kept their interest by inventing competitions and telling them stories. After a full year she left of her own accord to become a nursery governess to four youngsters in a large house in Surbiton, some 10 miles west of the family home.

For the first time in years, Enid was truly happy. Her employers treated her as one of the family. The children adored her and, as Surbiton was then almost a rural area, she could enjoy the birds and wild flowers of the country when she went for a walk. She had completely broken away from the restrictions of her own home and never saw her mother, although she kept in touch with her father through occasional visits to his City office. She did not, perhaps would not, meet the woman he lived with.

It must, therefore, have been a devastating blow when he suddenly died of a heart attack at the age of fifty. Yet she did not attend the funeral and never mentioned this fact to her close acquaintances. Perhaps she thought Thomas's mistress, who she felt had supplanted her in his affections, might attend and she did not want to risk a confrontation. More probably, her behaviour was caused by a mixture of two quite different feelings. In her more mature years, Enid had an almost brutal acceptance of facts that could not be altered. When one of her favourite publishers, a friend of long standing, died suddenly, she telephoned me as her agent when the news broke and asked, 'Who is going to take over?' There was no word of sympathy for him or his family. He was dead, someone else would have to run the show, let's get on with it – that was her attitude.

Along with the tough approach, there was a softer, conflicting side to Enid. Her avoidance of her father's funeral could have been a case of that old adage, 'If you ignore it, it may go away'. Indeed, if you refuse to look in that particular direction, you might even delude yourself that 'it' is not there at all. In her later years, many of the feelings she had suppressed for so long came back to haunt her, but while she was still young and strong and aspiring they could be waved aside.

For the next two years, she was a dynamo of industry. Not only, as governess, did she teach the four energetic youngsters – and from all accounts taught them well – but in her off-duty hours she was pouring out poems, short stories, some of them aimed at adults, and nature studies. At this time, she realized her forte was writing for children. Indeed, she tried out various drafts on her pupils and apparently quite often amended them depending on their reactions. And she was gradually getting known in the book world. In 1921 and 1922 various of her short stories and poems appeared in the *Saturday Westminster Review*, the *Bystander*, the *Londoner*, *Passing Show*, and other magazines of the period. Her first book, *Child Whispers*, a collection of poems published by the small firm of Saville in 1922, received some good reviews. The following year, Saville's published two books, her total output, and in 1924 a fourth. But in the latter year a new publisher entered the scene – Newnes, which brought out her other two titles for that year. Saville's were never again to publish a book by Enid Blyton. They had done their bit in launching her and getting her noticed. Now, more powerful machines were available to take her further. In 1922 she earned well over £300 for her published work, in 1924 over £500, and in 1925 over £1,200.

From 1920 for about the next forty years, three large groups dominated the popular magazine and 'spin-off' books market. They were Amalgamated Press, Odhams and Newnes. In 1923, Hugh Alexander Pollock, the son of an antique bookseller in Ayr, was appointed editor of the Newnes book department. He had had an outstanding war record, ending as a major with the Distinguished Service Order. His photographs show him as having a handsome, sensitive face; in the pictures taken soon after the war the viewer can almost sense the ravages of life in a front-line trench, where a man might welcome a wound as 'a ticket to Blighty', away from the risk of death. He was married, but his wife had left him for another man during the war and – perhaps from delicacy? – he had not yet commenced divorce proceedings.

Enid Blyton had submitted various stories to Newnes and Hugh Pollock must have seen some merit in them because he wrote to suggest she should write for children a book on London Zoo. After they met they were soon on more than 'author-editor' terms. Enid was then very much a Jane Eyre figure; apart from her two brothers, she had met relatively few men and almost none of marriageable age. In those morally stricter times, single unattached women did not go around unchaperoned or, far worse, have short-lived affairs. One might have expected the inexperienced woman, who was already twenty-six, to throw herself at the debonair ex-army officer, who was sophisticated enough to know most of the good clubs and restaurants – one of his favourites being Rules in Maiden Lane, about 50 yards from the Newnes building. But Enid appears to have been somewhat calculating in her approach. Again like Jane Eyre, she was not prepared to go beyond friendship with Hugh while he was still officially married to someone else. The divorce finally went through in the spring of 1924 and Enid, having given up her post as governess rather abruptly, married Hugh at Bromley Register Office near the end of August 1924, a couple of weeks after her twenty-seventh birthday.

The next ten years were almost idyllic. They took a flat in Chelsea. Although Hugh was away all day at work, Enid was never lonely. Apart from her own prolific writings, she edited three volumes of *The Teachers' Treasury* for Newnes in 1926 and also a volume of *Sunny Stories for Little Folk*. The previous year, she had earned £1,200 (equivalent to about £50,000 in today's terms), which was probably as much as, perhaps more than, Hugh's salary from Newnes. Enid was still much in love with him, but she must have realized that she was now 'a woman of independent means'.

A countryman born and bred, Hugh began to feel hemmed in at the Chelsea flat and hankered after the rural life. Enid had already proved that she could write almost anywhere and she too felt the tug of the countryside. They found a newly built small house in Shortlands Road, Beckenham. What is now a suburban sprawl was then on the edge of open fields and small farms. Enid was back on home soil, within a few minutes' walk of old friends and only a mile or so from her mother's house, although there is no record of their meeting. Shortlands station was ideally placed to transport Hugh to and from his London office. Elfin Cottage, as they named their home, was a happy home. Already, as she was to do increasingly throughout her writing career, Enid made 'copy' out of the move. She had been commissioned to write a regular column for *Teachers' World* and throughout 1926 several of these pieces decribed various aspects of settling in, laying out the garden and so forth.

Towards the end of that year, *Teachers' World* (26 October 1926) issued a special supplement containing a full-page interview with Enid Blyton. It was signed 'H.A', Hugh's initials. The last question he put to her was tongue in cheek. He had been 'meaning to ask it for a long time: why must she work so hard when she had a husband, home, happiness and peace?' Enid's answer was, 'So long as one child tells me that my work brings him pleasure, just so long shall I go on writing.' Already, her writing had become a crusade for her and the feeling of fulfilling a noble obligation would increase as the years progressed.

Hugh's interview article was read by teachers throughout the country, many of whom must have shown it to their pupils. She was already becoming established as an important figure in the children's magazine and book fields. She received thousands of letters and postcards a year from her fans, all of which she replied to assiduously – a practice she followed as long as she was mentally capable. Her replies were all handwritten, as indeed up to then were her scripts. But in 1927, at Hugh's insistence, she learned to type by the old 'finger and thumb' method. One would have thought that an experienced pianist would have preferred touch typing, and she did indeed become highly dextrous in typing at speed. Right to the last, her letters of reply and cards, being on a personal level, were always handwritten.

Life went on happily at Elfin Cottage for the next few years. As there was a maid to do the housework, Enid was free to write while Hugh was away at his office. The couple enjoyed quiet seaside holidays and went occasionally to the theatre and cinema but did little entertaining. They seemed pleasantly wrapped up in each another. Enid had the professional writer's eye for making use of actual events to furbish her articles, although she had a tendency to glamourize and improve on Nature. For example, when touring by car in Scotland, their holiday was plagued by continual heavy rain, engine breakdowns and punctures. According to her subsequent column, the weather had been sunny throughout and 'a good time was had by all'.

The one thing they lacked to make the family complete was a child. After months of trying to conceive, Enid consulted a gynaecologist during the early part of 1928, to be told that her womb was under-developed. She underwent hormone treatment for several months, but to no effect. Her life at different times was to be laced with irony – the woman who had already become a children's favourite apparently could not produce a child of her own.

T W O

WAR AND
RE-MARRIAGE

The suburbs of southern London were already creeping further south and, in Enid's words, 'a great new arterial road' was planned in the neighbourhood of Elfin Cottage. She and Hugh decided to move and quite soon found Old Thatch, a large Tudor cottage in Bourne End, Buckinghamshire, a short walk from the River Thames. It had an extensive garden with an orchard, a small brook, and an ancient well. Enid was now in her element. *Teachers' World* had given her extra space and she filled it with short stories, competitions, and a 'letter' purporting to be from the paw of Bobs, her pet fox terrier. The dog had been with her for three years, since it was a few months old, and had been referred to regularly during those years. In the new house, it soon had a 'readership' all of its own. Hugh, versed in the ways of publishing, was shrewd enough to let *Teachers' World*, the weekly *Sunny Stories* and other periodicals publish Enid's writings under licence – a practice known in the trade as 'First British Serial Rights' – while she retained the copyrights. By such means, she was able to 'cannibalize' the material for appropriate books at a later date. In 1933 Enid issued a booklet entitled *Letters from Bobs* and sold it direct to the public for threepence a copy (which would be about £1 today). Within the first week, 10,000 copies were sold. One hopes Bobs received a few extra dog biscuits for the success of 'his' book.

Enid's young readers were not confined to a well-to-do, middle-class circle. Poorer children from the 'smoke stack' towns and cities of the industrial Midlands and North were also avid readers. Indeed, part of the fascination for them must have been the images of fruit trees and flowers and green lawns which she conjured up for them on the printed page. Her prose style and general approach to writing are discussed in a later chapter but, just as Enid's personality and warmth were displayed in teaching children on a one-to-one basis, these characteristics were also apparent in her writing technique. The young

reader could feel that she was talking straight to –
and only to – him or her.

At barely thirty years of age, Enid Blyton was
already a woman of power and influence in the
world of children. When she announced that Bobs
had 'become' a member of the Tail Waggers Club,
there were so many new applicants wishing to join
that the club presented Bobs with a silver medal.
Again, when she recommended a private anti-litter
society in both *Teachers' World* and *Sunny Stories*, the
rush to join was overwhelming. Within a matter of
months, there had been 25,000 new members and
further applications rolled in for many weeks
thereafter. But secretly she must have felt
incomplete. She had Hugh's protective love,
although his promotion into a yet more responsible
job at Newnes often kept him working late hours;
she had new friends in the neighbourhood to
socialize with at tennis and bridge parties and an
attractive old house and garden to enjoy. She had
hundreds of thousands of young friends spread
around the country and, increasingly, overseas. The
one thing she lacked was a child of her own.

In October 1930, Enid and Hugh took a cruise to
Madeira and the Canary Islands. It must have taken

some persuading on his part because she had all the prejudices of the 'little Englander'. 'Abroad' was viewed with suspicion: the scenery might be acceptable but the local people ate too much rich food, drank wine, and talked too fast in a strange language; worse, their standards of sanitation were deplorable. According to her many descriptive columns in *Teachers' World* – as usual, she milked each experience to the last drop – she appears to have enjoyed the voyage, in spite of a storm in the Bay of Biscay. But the Union Jack still flew proudly at the top of the flagpole. As one of the columns put it, 'I know that, no matter where I go or what I see in other countries, I shall always love England best.'

Yet something had changed. On their return from the cruise Enid suffered bouts of nausea in the mornings and consulted her doctor, who thought she might be pregnant. A few weeks later, during a second visit, he confirmed the opinion. In July 1931, she gave birth to her first daughter, Gillian.

As the 1930s progressed Enid also acquired new publishers to cope with her expanding output. To the long-standing trio of Newnes, Evans Brothers and Nelson's, she added Methuen, Birn Brothers,

Wheaton, Warne, Frederick Muller, W. & A.K. Johnston, Blackwell, Arnold and Country Life, which was part of the Newnes group. The main staple of her writing was fiction – collections of short stories for sub-teenagers – but there were also retold classics, school stories, nature studies, Bible stories, poems and plays. To some extent she 'cannibalized' her contributions to *Sunny Stories* and *Teachers' World*, but much was original.

Her home life was cossetted by a chauffeur-gardener, a cook-general, and a succession of housemaids to look after Gillian, and from 1935 onwards her second daughter Imogen. She was inclined to be brutal when dealing with the junior staff. One mistake – or apparent mistake – and they were dismissed. Her true attitude to domestic servants was then a far cry from the almost sugary approach adopted in her stories.

The year 1934 was a difficult one for Hugh. Already stretched by being in control of a large and expanding department at Newnes, he was now personally looking after several eminent authors, Winston Churchill in particular. Churchill was writing *The World Crisis*, which was to appear in partwork format. Hugh had to visit Chartwell from time to time to discuss illustrations and a little 'touching up' of the text with the man he idolized. Barbara Stoney has suggested that re-living the drama and awfulness of the First World War through listening to Churchill's views in person and reading his powerful text drove Hugh to the edge of a nervous breakdown. It is more likely that Hugh Pollock, a highly conscientious man, just could not delegate this important new work, which stretched him beyond reasonable limits.

Enid, it seems, did not afford him the rest and relaxation he so badly needed on returning to Old Thatch each evening. Having rattled off her word quota through the daytime, she looked forward to a game of bridge or a tennis party in the summer months, once her husband was home. He would have to socialize when he must have been aching for a deep armchair, a stiff drink and something amusing on the 'wireless'.

In mid-1935 Bobs was dying painfully but Enid refused to accept the fact or have him put down. He died that November and was buried in the garden in an unmarked grave. The fact was concealed from readers and Bobs went on 'writing' his letters for quite a few years thereafter.

Under considerable and increasing stress at
work, Hugh was drinking more spirits than usual to
allay that stress and, constitutionally, he also had
what used to be termed 'a weak chest'. This
combination caused him, in the late spring of 1938,
to suffer a serious bout of pneumonia and he was
rushed to hospital. There was then no penicillin,
other antibiotics, nebulizers or special inhalants to
ease the tortured lungs; the patient had, almost
literally, to sweat it out. Hugh was on the danger list
and his brother was hurriedly summoned from
Scotland. The crisis even dammed Enid's typed
outpourings for a few days. But, Hugh must have
possessed inner physical as well as mental strength –
he rallied and after four weeks in hospital was
discharged, cured.

There had been an additional bone of contention
between Enid and Hugh. She had struck up a
friendship with an efficient and well-qualified nurse,
Dorothy Richards, who had been called in to look
after Imogen soon after her birth. Dorothy
Richards, who was unmarried, was an attractive,
dark-haired woman, and so resembled Enid that she
could almost have been mistaken for her sister. In
any event, a deep and abiding affection grew up

between the two women. Dorothy accompanied the family on holiday to the Isle of Wight in 1936 and in her spare time she often called or stayed at Old Thatch. Hugh must have begun to feel that his wife's off-duty hours and interests were being taken up with a feminine rival. Before the war, the husband was supposed to 'rule the roost'. Now that Enid was wealthy in her own right and becoming far better known to the public than he would ever be, Hugh must have felt their roles had been smartly reversed.

Enid and Dorothy together decided that the Pollock family should leave Old Thatch and seek a new home – a decision that did not endear Hugh to the place, when found. It was a detached house in Penn Road, half a mile from the centre of Beaconsfield, then a rural village. Enid invited her many young readers to choose a name; Green Hedges was the favourite by a large majority. The family moved in days before the Munich Crisis broke when Chamberlain was cheered as he disembarked from the aircraft, waving a piece of paper and uttering the mistaken prophecy, 'Peace in our time!'. Hugh felt unsettled – and not only by the move to new surroundings. He still gave Enid his love and affection and sought the same from her in return. But he shared Churchill's forebodings and, as 1939 progressed, felt all the more certain there would be a major war. Enid, happy in her new home, acquiring new readers all the time and surrounded by care and attention, adopted the role of an ostrich. Bobs, long dead, was now 'barking away' in the columns of *Sunny Stories* and Enid appears to have accepted the same make-believe outlook.

Paper for printing books was one of the early casualties of the war. Previously, the amount supplied was only rationed by the depth of the respective publisher's purse, but now there was strict rationing. Each publisher was given a quota, a percentage of the amount the firm had used in the last full year before hostilities began. The initial quota was 50 per cent, raised to 60 per cent in October 1939. It remained at that level until early 1946 when it was raised to 75 per cent, with an extra 10 per cent to be used strictly for export. The quota system was eventually abandoned in March 1949. Conscientious publishers felt that they could not devote the bulk of their limited stocks to a few popular authors, which meant that

Enid had to spread her wares that much wider. As well as the half dozen or so 'Old Faithfuls', new names emerge in her wartime and immediate postwar publishers: *News Chronicle*, a newspaper connected to the Newnes Group, Macmillan, Hodder & Stoughton, Brockhampton Press, a Hodder & Stoughton subsidiary, Werner Laurie, Lutterworth Press, National Magazine Company, Latimer House, Pitkin, Harold Hill, Gifford, Sidgwick & Jackson and William Collins. This list also included Sampson Low, who were to be the publishers of the Noddy books.

Momentous events also occurred on the home front in the first two years of the war. Hugh felt that he must set his military skill and experience at the service of his country. At the age of fifty-one he was beyond the call-up limits; he had given much in the First World War but his patriotic urge made him rally again to the trumpet's call, greatly to Enid's chagrin. Naturally enough, she wanted her husband at her side, not defending an area many miles away. She still firmly believed in ignoring an unpleasant situation in the hope that it might go way. Besides, with an ample fruit and vegetable garden, attentive servants, eager publishers and being a safe distance from the Luftwaffe's 'bomb alley', the unpleasantness of war really did seem to diminish, if not disappear.

But it was one thing to volunteer and quite another to be called up. The 'phoney war' was on and bureaucracy was overwhelmed by the rush of volunteers. Hugh did not get his call-up until well into 1940. He used the time to co-write an important book on military tactics. When the call did finally come, he served briefly at Catterick Camp and was then posted to Dorking in Surrey as commandant of No. 1 War Office School for Home Guard officers. It was an important and responsible posting. Britain was fighting alone. Troops were urgently needed in the Middle East and the Western Desert, since Mussolini had brought Italy into the war. The more the Home Guard was ready and able to defend the homeland from invasion, the more fighting soldiers could be released for overseas service. So successful was Hugh at training the Home Guard officers that his name, he later discovered, was put on the Nazis' priority list for extermination.

Dorking is about 40 miles by road from Beaconsfield. Petrol for private use was severely rationed but a rich author with a chauffeur had fewer problems than most. There is no record that Enid ever visited Dorking during the eighteen months or so that Hugh was commandant there. As she only published nine books in 1941 as opposed to thirteen in 1940 (two under the pseudonym Mary Pollock), she could have had time to spare. There seems to have been a flaming row between them when Hugh returned on Christmas leave in 1940. With the children away at school during the daytime and no other adult at home in the evenings, Enid may have sought the company of various unattached men who lived in or near Beaconsfield. If so, these would almost certainly have been innocent relationships but Hugh, whose first wife had been unfaithful to him when he was absent on duty in the First World War, must have had qualms.

As commandant of the War Office School, he ran a course on the handling of mortars. On one occasion, there was a premature explosion and a piece of shrapnel penetrated the side of his face. Blood welled up and he was rushed to an emergency ward. A member of his staff rang Enid, broke the bad news and offered to book her into a

Dorking hotel, adding that the Colonel's driver would meet her at the station.

After all these years, Enid's reply is remembered verbatim. She did not ask how bad the accident was but said, 'Oh, but I couldn't possibly come to Dorking! You see, I'm absolutely no good in a sick room, and I hate hospitals. I know it sounds awful, but I really do. . . . If he's going to be ill for some time, could you let me know how he gets on? Perhaps you could ring me every day – keep me informed, if you wouldn't mind? The best time of day to ring me is in the evening.'

Fortunately for him, Hugh made a fairly quick and complete recovery in spite of his wife's somewhat tepid response. Visiting one's husband when he may be gravely ill does interfere with publishing deadlines.

Within months, the eighteen-year-old marriage, already under stress, was to be shattered. Dorothy Richards arranged to take Enid on a short holiday to her sister's home in Devon. Some doctors from London happened to be in the locality on a golfing tour. A bridge party took place – and Enid met Kenneth Darrell Waters, a surgeon. He was seven years older than she was, on the short side, but vigorous in his movements — having not yet developed the arthritis that was to plague him in later years — and had a powerful personality. He was profoundly deaf, having experienced a shell burst during the Battle of Jutland when he was a junior naval doctor, but, with determination and the aid of hearing devices, he had worked his way up to become a senior surgeon. The rapport between Enid and himself was instantaneous. Shortly after the holiday, Enid took the lease of a London flat in Dorothy's name; it was to be a regular rendezvous for her and Kenneth.

When word reached Hugh that there was 'another man', he decided to divorce Enid. He was already falling in love with Ida Crowe, a struggling but later successful novelist, whom he had first met at Newnes before the war and who was now stationed in his area. Enid came to hear of that relationship and said *she* would divorce *him*. His chivalry always to the fore, he agreed to be the 'guilty party' (a requirement for divorce in those days) provided he had regular access to his two daughters and there was no recrimination on either side. He was over-trusting and after all those years still did not comprehend in depth the character of his soon to be ex-wife. Enid did not comply with the arrangement and he never saw Gillian or Imogen again.

Enid would have been a successful writer in any circumstances – there is no stopping an avalanche – but there is little doubt that Hugh expedited her career. Without the backing of Newnes and its wide grasp of the juvenile market, she might have had to wait some years before reaching a large readership.

In our prurient and celebrity-hunting times, there would be headlines in the popular press, blaring out the details of a famous children's author's divorce. Fortunately for Enid's relationship with her more puritanical publishers, booksellers and librarians of the day, not to mention the mothers of her readers, 'there was a war on' when her decree nisi was granted at the end of 1942. The headlines were dominated by the Eighth Army's victories as it pushed Rommel's Afrika Korps back into Tunisia. Kenneth also had a marriage to untangle himself from and it was not until October 1943 that he and Enid became man and wife. A few days later, Hugh married Ida Crowe at a different London register office.

THREE

SUCCESS – WITH A SAD ENDING

Much of Enid's appeal to Kenneth, apart from her physical charms and, of course, her substantial income, was her ability to converse with him. As a trained teacher, she knew how to pitch her voice high enough to be easily heard by him. He was – and remained throughout his life – immensely proud of her achievements and jealous to defend her reputation as an author. In 1952, he even threatened to sue the BBC over a humorous aside made in a radio series. But he was also a bit of a domestic despot. Apparently, there were numerous clashes in the early months of their marriage. Enid, with a gentle first husband, had been used to getting her own way – and she now came up against someone with a will as firm as, perhaps firmer than, her own. Overall, the couple appear to have been intensely happy; the one dark cloud occurred early in 1945 when Enid became pregnant and then miscarried. The child would have been a boy.

In 1942, Hodder & Stoughton had published *Five on a Treasure Island*, the first of what was to become the second best-known series of children's books in her vast output. Seven years later, in 1949, the best known of all, about Noddy, was to be launched with *Little Noddy Goes to Toyland*. The series's *accouchement* was unusual, to say the least. Enid happened to call at the Mayfair offices of Sampson Low and was shown the drawings of a Dutchman named Van der Beek, who signed his artwork simply as 'Beek'. She was immediately struck with the childish charm of the drawings and said aloud, 'I could write a story around those'. David White, the senior director of Sampson Low, was present and had the wit to reply, 'Why don't you?', which is how it all started. Enid even agreed to accept only a 5 per cent royalty, a third of her normal rate, provided that Van der Beek received the same. There was an argument for keeping the overall royalty on the low side because the book would be heavily illustrated and the four-colour printing process was expensive. Sadly, Van der Beek died within a few years of the highly successful launch. For the next eighteen years, Sampson Low paid a series of illustrators comparatively small sums to reproduce the Van der Beek 'style' while they pocketed what would have been his very substantial royalties.

A thrusting entrepreneur named William Harvey had taken over Purnell & Sons, the sleepy printing firm in Somerset, and turned it into a big and successful outfit. In order to provide input for the 'hungry' machines, he went on a buying spree of publishers, picking up Macdonald & Co., Juvenile Productions, Sampson Low and even the esoteric list of John Lehmann. Enid and Kenneth came to know Clifford Gibbs, one of Harvey's directors, who had played rugby football for England. He had a brother working in a City stockbroking firm, whose senior partner was Eric W. Rogers. The latter was introduced to the famous author and her husband, and he and Kenneth became close friends and soon he was appointed their broker and financial adviser. Enid and Kenneth were both to die happy in his friendship and knew nothing of his machinations, some of which are revealed in Chapter 5.

He advised them to set up a limited liability company, to which all Enid's existing and future copyrights would be assigned. The advice was quite sound because by 1949 she had over 250 titles in print, the sale of foreign rights was increasing and taxation of individuals was growing harsher with each Budget under the postwar Labour government. The company was formed in 1950 under the name of Darrell Waters Limited – Kenneth was already asserting his masculine domination. He was also to persuade Enid, who perhaps did not require much persuasion, to have her two daughters' surnames changed by deed poll to Darrell Waters. The 'Darrell' was a later affectation, as at King's School, Rochester, where he was educated, he was known merely as Waters, K.F.D. When the Trocadero group acquired the company in 1996, the name was changed to what it should always have been – Enid Blyton Limited.

The other directors of the newly formed company were Arnold Thirlby, Enid's solicitor, and John Basden, an independent accountant whose other clients included Laurence Olivier and Ralph Richardson. They used to meet about once a month at the corner table in the Savoy Restaurant, which

'Wing Commander' Rogers (he had not dropped his wartime title) occupied every day, presumably at the company's expense. He would arrive at the River Entrance in his Bentley with the personalized number-plate EWR 1. Enid attended the lunches on most occasions and, when she invited me to become her literary agent at the beginning of 1953, I was also a regular guest. Champagne would be drunk, a notable claret would accompany the main course and cigars and brandy provided for the men afterwards. They would talk across Enid and in a sense down to her, treating her almost like a favourite niece who was still feeling her way in a man's world. Without the largesse arising from her mighty labours, none of them would have been living off the fat of the land in this manner.

For Enid, the decade 1951–60 was to be one of consolidation and expansion. By 1945 she had already given up her long-standing column in *Teachers' World* and in 1952 her association with *Sunny Stories* ended after twenty-eight years. She had plans for a magazine of her own, the *Enid Blyton Magazine*, whose first issue appeared in the spring of 1953. For the next six and a half years until she closed it in the autumn of 1959, the fortnightly magazine was virtually all Enid's 'own work', comprising short stories, articles, puzzles and games. Apart from widening yet further her band of devoted readers, the magazine sponsored and helped various worthwhile charities for children.

At the suggestion of her publishers, Hodder & Stoughton, a Famous Five Club was created in 1952. The Famous Five books, published at regular yearly intervals since 1942, had thousands of readers who must have felt a close kinship with the characters, not least 'George'. Some of them proposed to start a special club, an idea that both Hodder's and Enid were enthusiastic about. With a peak membership of over 200,000, the club raised large sums for charities, especially Great Ormond Street Hospital for Sick Children. Enid may have been reviled at the time by the more aesthetic of literary critics, but her devoted fans knew better and she achieved more in good works than any column in *Encounter* was likely to do.

Early in 1954, Enid sought my opinion as her agent. Did I think she was capable of writing a children's pantomime? Agents can be prone to flattery when their important clients are concerned, but my response was wholly sincere. In my view, I said, if she put her mind to it, she could write just about anything for the juvenile market. A couple of weeks later, the book and lyrics of the *Noddy in Toyland* pantomime landed on my desk. I then had two young sons of my own aged six and four and I knew at once it would be popular with them. With Enid's permission, I passed the script to Bertie Meyer, a producer of great repute, who quickly assembled a composer for the music, Philip Green, and a director, André van Gyseghen. A firm booking was also made for matinées at the vast Stoll Theatre in London over the Christmas holiday period.

Bertie Meyer, an imposingly large figure with snowy white hair, was then in his seventies. As a very young man, he had produced a play for the great actor Sir Henry Irving. Kenneth, in his querulous piping tone, complained about Bertie's age: he was bound to drop dead in the middle of rehearsals; the whole thing would be a disaster; he was far too old for the job. Having suspected that Kenneth might take such a stand, Bertie had gone to his Harley Street doctor for a thorough overhaul, which proved him to be in excellent health. I waved the diagnosis in Kenneth's face and Enid for once put her foot down. She said she liked and trusted

Bertie and wanted him as her producer. The ironic outcome was that within fifteen years she and Kenneth would both be dead but Bertie, then in his late eighties, was still going strong, mentally alert and physically quite vigorous.

The Stoll, now used for television audiences, was then the theatre with the largest seating capacity in London. It was sold out for every single performance of the pantomime season for the Christmas holidays 1954–5. For the next six years or so, the *Noddy in Toyland* pantomime enjoyed full houses at various West End theatres.

In September 1955, Independent Television was set up in direct competition with the BBC, which hitherto had enjoyed a monopoly. Norman Collins, the well-known novelist, along with his agent, A.D. Peters, formed a small company, High Definition Studios, to make TV films for young children. The first name they wanted was Enid Blyton and, in particular, her creation, Noddy, about whom they wished to make a series of short puppet films. ITV had been given only a few months to be up and running and it was not unusual in those days to be discussing likely programmes with a director of, say, Associated Rediffusion while the carpet in his office was being laid around one's feet. When Enid, Kenneth and I arrived at the High Definition office to watch the puppets in action there was indeed a carpet on the floor but no desk and only two rickety looking chairs. In order to get a proper view, we all had to lie on the floor on our stomachs and gaze at the dolls while the puppeteer made them dance a few feet away. Enid in her mink coat thoroughly enjoyed the escapade; Kenneth with his arthritis was less happy at the unaccustomed posture. The Noddy puppet programmes were put out by Associated Television on Sunday afternoons and achieved very good ratings.

By now, the demand for merchandising was becoming intense. Hitherto, it had been dealt with on a hit or miss basis, usually by the publisher of the relevant books. I had no expertise in the merchandising field and proposed that a specialist should be brought in to deal with this. I knew that a debonair New Zealander, Walter Tuckwell, who had run the Walt Disney London office, was about to set up his own firm and I introduced him to Enid and Kenneth — and to Eric Rogers. Tuckwell produced some good results in the short time he was 'on board' and he trained Victor Broadribb of Sampson

Low, the Noddy publishers, in the crafts of merchandising. But apparently his smooth talking aroused jealousy – or perhaps fear – in the heart of Eric Rogers, who could be quite a smooth talker himself, and he was soon cast out.

Buoyed by her theatrical success with the Noddy pantomime, Enid wrote a straight stage play featuring the Famous Five. It too had a couple of well-attended Christmas seasons in the West End, which led indirectly to an offer from the Children's Film Foundation to back a screen version. In the 1950s the major cinema chains used to put on special children's programmes on Saturday mornings. Rank Screen Services shot the film, directed by H.G. Wells's son, Frank, in Enid's favourite county of Dorset.

Great success is often accompanied by a counterblast. In January 1958 Colin Welch wrote a vituperative piece in *Encounter* about Noddy – 'the most egocentric, joyless, snivelling and pious anti-hero in the history of British fiction'. Librarians across the country tried to avoid stocking the Blyton books on one or both of two grounds: firstly, that they did not exercise sufficiently the minds of their young readers; secondly, that they were racist and class-ridden. Her very profligacy as an author gave rise to the rumour that 'Enid Blyton' was in fact a team of writers tapping away at their respective keyboards. Enid was intensely proud of her work, and would not have allowed anyone else to interfere or pass off their works as hers and in the twenty years I saw her frequently there was never the slightest hint of another hand at work. But the rumour became so strong in the late 1950s that Arnold Thirlby, her lawyer, had to take legal action against a South African librarian who kept on repeating it in public. This resulted in an apology being made in open court.

Flushed with the huge and continuing success of her juvenile plays, Enid secretly decided to attempt a play for adults. Under the deprecatory pen-name of Justin Geste, the script entitled *The Summer Storm* landed on my desk without warning. The plot was banal and 'theatrical' in the wrong sense of that word. I knew in my heart that it was hopeless but, duty bound, showed it to Bertie Meyer, who in turn had André van Gyseghen read it privately. Diplomatically, for they both liked and admired Enid, they rejected it, and I had the difficult task of persuading her to withdraw it, which she did. From long years of experience, she knew exactly what appealed to children but perhaps by now she was unable to make the imaginative leap required to write in a way which would appeal to adults.

Kenneth retired from his post as senior surgeon at St Stephen's Hospital, Fulham in 1957. Thereafter, he could spend all his waking hours wrapping an even closer protective cocoon around his famous wife, or, as her publishers and others might have put it, interfering in matters he did not fully understand. A keen golfer, he arranged for the company to buy a golf course at Swanage, where he and Enid would play during their holidays. His arthritis had spread to the hips as well as the neck and he charged around the links in an electric cart, much to the peril of himself and anyone else within range. At other times, he and Enid would play at the local Beaconsfield course. During a round of golf there a few months after his retirement, Enid complained of breathlessness. Kenneth rushed her home and sent for a cardiologist, who took various tests and cleared her of any heart condition. In his opinion her symptoms were the result of a form of indigestion brought on by all those hours spent hunched over a typewriter. But for weeks afterwards, Kenneth maintained – and told the two daughters, Gillian and Imogen, and a few close friends – that Enid had suffered a minor heart attack. Whether he felt she really had or whether he used it as an excuse to make her slow down and cut out unnecessary activities we shall probably never know. Enid, remembering that her beloved father had died of a heart attack when he was ten years younger than she now was, must have had premonitions as her husband spread the wrong word out of the best of motives.

In 1960, Gordon Landsborough, a publisher of real flair and imagination who was well versed in the paperback market, approached me as a literary agent with a novel idea. The publishers of paperbacks were then aiming exclusively at adult readers. Puffin Books, an offshoot of Penguin, was working on an 'up market' series of titles for children but there was no mass market juvenile house. Youngsters were then, he argued, getting at least 5s (25p) as their weekly pocket money. A paperback book cost half a crown (12½p). Whereas for generations children had relied on their parents to buy books for them, now they could afford to buy their own. Enid Blyton, he considered, was the key to the operation. If he could launch his planned Armada books with half a dozen of her titles, he would change the face of children's publishing.

On her own territory, Enid showed impeccable judgement. Although Kenneth and Eric Rogers complained that she was rushing things, she at once saw the validity of Landsborough's plan. She persuaded her hardback publishers to release a bunch of titles to Armada Books, which flourished. Indeed, the company thrived to such an extent that it was eventually bought out by Collins and absorbed into its children's department in Glasgow. No doubt the development would have arisen sooner or later but, coming when it did, it helped to keep Enid's sales flourishing in the years when her annual output was beginning to tail off.

As 1960 approached its end, Enid was a happy and fulfilled woman, in spite of the so-called 'heart attack' three years earlier. Gillian was married with a growing family, Imogen had completed her university course at St Andrew's, Kenneth was a devoted companion, and her many books were selling in ever increasing quantities. The sun was shining brightly, but the clouds were beginning to roll up.

Enid Blyton in her twenties.

Enid Blyton reading *Round the Clock Stories* in the library at her home, Green Hedges, 1945.

Enid in the garden at Green Hedges with her second husband, Kenneth Darrell Waters.

A party to launch one of Enid's books at Hatchards, 1952. Left to right: George Greenfield, Clarence Hatry (chairman of Hatchards), Joan Werner Laurie and Enid Blyton.

Noddy and Big Ears taking a drive in Toyland from an early Noddy book.

Enid Blyton surrounded by Noddy merchandise.

A dust jacket typical of those used for Enid Blyton's early publications. This
was the cover for *Last Term at Malory Towers*, published in 1951.

Enid relaxing at home with her Siamese cat.

Enid at work with her
portable typewriter
balanced on her knee
and a cat at her feet.

Enid's eldest daughter Gillian Baverstock with Norman Wright, editor of the *Enid Blyton Literary Society Journal*, at the Enid Blyton Day held in Hertfordshire, 1994.

Another early dust jacket for Enid Blyton's *The Sea of Adventure*, published in 1948.

FOUR

'SHE THOUGHT AS A CHILD'

In her prime Enid Blyton was a striking-looking woman. Somewhat above medium height, she had dark hair, bunched in tight curls on either side of her face, a reddish complexion and fine glowing eyes. There was a singing, almost a chirruping, quality to her speaking voice. On subjects which she knew well, such as natural history, gardening, the likes and dislikes of young readers and the wiles of publishers, she sounded authoritative, indeed didactic. In her own small circles of friends she was comfortable, but in a wider social gathering often strangely ill at ease, almost flustered.

The winter 1996 issue of *The Enid Blyton Literary Society Magazine*, which is edited by Tony Summerfield and Norman Wright and published twice yearly, contained some fascinating memories from Doris Cox, who joined the Darrell Waters family at Green Hedges in 1946 as house parlour maid and remained Enid's loyal and devoted companion to the very end. Many of her apparently naïve observations were very apt: 'Sometimes Dr and Mrs Waters gave dinner parties. Doctors from the hospital used to come and sometimes publishers. Only men came. Mrs Waters was usually the only woman. She used to wear a red velvet dress with rubies and emeralds. There were red candles on the table and the curtains were red too. She loved red.'

There was a strong sense of coiled-up energy about Enid. One felt she should be tapping away furiously at her typewriter or scribbling cards in reply to letters from her countless young admirers or digging the garden or striding after her ball on the Dorset golf course which her company had bought; anything rather than waste her time in banal chatting.

Until her last few years, she had the most extraordinary memory. As I mentioned in Chapter 1, she replied to all correspondents, whether it be a six year old or the chairman of a large publishing house, by handwritten cards and letters. She took no copies and, as far as could be seen, had no filing system at Green Hedges. And yet she could telephone me and ask whether there had been any new developments over a query for some obscure South American translation rights which had occurred more than six months before.

An author who wrote on average more than fifteen books every year needed a good memory. With a prolific series like *The Famous Five* or *The Secret Seven* or even *Noddy in Toyland*, Enid Blyton had to memorize not only the characters' names, including the minor ones, and their characteristics but also all the previous storylines, to avoid repeating herself. She attracted readers across a ten-year age group, from three to four year olds at one end to those reaching puberty at the other. She regaled them with a wide variety of subjects and themes, including fairy stories, nature stories, Bible stories, fantasy and adventure stories. She could, and did, switch from one to the other with alarming ease.

In her lifetime, the publishing world had a simple axiom. Authors who make a lot of money for themselves make a lot of money for their publishers (it no longer holds true, with the coming of wildly inflated advances for 'big' authors, which may leave the author richer but the publisher far poorer). But, naturally enough, the Blyton publishers, all twenty of them at her peak, doted on her and she could be correspondingly strict with them. She would not take an advance on account of royalties, a gesture which publishers much appreciated as their capital was therefore not locked up, but as a balancing factor she insisted on a first printing of no fewer than 25,000 copies. Only once did she break her rule of 'no advances' and that was with *The Big Enid Blyton Book*, published by Paul Hamlyn in 1961. The advance was £5,000 – over £60,000 in today's currency – and, ironically, it turned out to be one of her least successful publications.

She also insisted on receiving a flat 15 per cent royalty based on the published price. Most children's authors have been offered somewhat harsh terms, particularly in the days when sensible advances led to generally higher royalty rates. These would usually start at 7½ per cent and gradually rise to 10 per cent, sometimes even to 12½ per cent if and when the sales reached, say, 15,000 copies. Blyton knew her worth and was quietly determined to get it.

And woe betide the publisher who failed to consult her over the choice of type face and size, the page layout, the dustjacket and the proposed illustrator. Of the last, she had her favourites, notably Eileen Soper. As she used to say, 'This is *my* book and it is going to look the way I want it to.' The errant publisher would suffer the worst fate of all – swiftly becoming an ex-publisher of Enid Blyton books. The fact is she knew children and appreciated the subconscious appeal of clear type and bright illustrations.

To write so many books over so many years, she had to become a creature of habit (her writing methods are discussed in Chapter 5). To maintain the output and answer all the letters from her young fans required her to spend the majority of her waking hours at the typewriter or desk, fountain pen in hand. She did not – indeed, would not – employ a secretary. The only breaks from the rigid routine occurred when she had lunch once a month or so at the Savoy with Kenneth and Eric Rogers, their stockbroking friend and adviser, or played golf with Kenneth, a keen exponent who had taught her the game.

She was caught in a kind of time-warp, ignorant of modern slang and idioms. On one occasion, she sent me, her agent, the script of a new Noddy story before the publishers had seen it. Noddy had done a good deed and had been rewarded with a penny. He then went round Toyland village, asking where he could spend his penny. I had to telephone her and with some embarrassment explain that 'spending a penny' was a euphemism for going to the lavatory, derived from the fact that, to enter a public cubicle, one had first to insert a penny in the slot. 'Really?' she said. 'How interesting. Well, I'll obviously have to alter that part.' And indeed she did.

Having spent over four years in and around the Middle East during the Second World War, I grew accustomed in rural villages to the sight of a blind-folded donkey plodding in circles around a deep well, turning the spindle that raised full buckets of water. The donkey must have thought it was making progress, not just returning each time to its starting point. I felt a similar sensation at times when reflecting on Enid's writing career. Apart from the breaks mentioned, her life had become con-centrated into a narrowing circle. She disliked 'abroad', which was strange and where the in-habitants would not at once realize who she was and what she stood for. Kenneth, however, liked to travel and he dearly wanted to try the thermal mud baths at Termi in northern Italy, which were reputed to benefit sufferers from rheumatism and arthritis. But Enid had grown used to Swanage in Dorset, where the hotel staff knew and much respected her. She had taken a cruise to Madeira in her younger days and a short round trip to New York by liner in 1948, but this was the extent of her overseas travel as an adult. The typewriter had become her centre. *Laborare* was not only *orare*, it was *vivere* as well.

Her daughters, Gillian and Imogen, had both been boarders at Benenden, one of the best public schools for girls, and so were absent during the crucial hours of creation. In 1989, Imogen published a memoir entitled *A Childhood at Green Hedges* which was widely serialized and which contained a poignant portrait of a neglectful mother and consequently miserable child. Ironically, it seemed, the woman who opened her arms to the world's children and offered them her love was too busy doing so to allow time for a kiss and a hug for her younger daughter. When mother was engrossed hour after hour over the typewriter, daughter had to keep well away and not make a disturbing noise. Gillian, on the other hand, describes her mother in retrospect as loving and attentive. The difference may lie in their dates of birth. In 1936, when Gillian was five, Enid published four books. In 1940, when Imogen was that age, she published thirteen.

Enid Blyton was perhaps best with children at a distance. On one occasion, she had agreed to give a short talk, followed by a signing session, at Hatchards Bookshop in Piccadilly. She was delayed by heavy traffic and arrived some fifteen minutes late. As the featured book was to be the latest Noddy book, the audience consisted mainly of five and six year olds. At that age, to sit still for two minutes with nothing to do is a torture, and by the time Enid entered the bookshop a juvenile riot had broken out. Children were climbing on – and falling off – the chairs, fights were in progress and there was screaming and yelling on all sides.

She sized up the situation at once, strode briskly on to the dais and said in a compelling voice, 'Children, I'm Enid Blyton. Now sit down at once! I'm going to tell you a story.' It was magical; the fighting and the din stopped abruptly. Meekly, the children climbed back on to their chairs, mouths slightly open, intent on every word from the great storyteller's lips.

Enid's first husband, Hugh, had introduced her writing to Newnes, the major magazine group, and she was soon writing for and then editing *Sunny Stories*. When the marriage broke up after more than fifteen years, he did his best to ensure a smooth dissolution. But, once the divorce was finalized, Hugh became an 'un-person' in Enid's eyes. He never saw his children again. Their surnames were changed by deed poll to Darrell Waters and Enid encouraged them to accept Kenneth as their 'father'.

A wartime Act of Parliament guaranteed that men and women demobilized at the end of the war would have the right to return to the jobs they left when they enlisted. In addition, Hugh had a contract 'on ice' with Newnes, but when he arrived to resume his post as Head of Serial Publications, he was bluntly informed that the contract was scrapped. He was given a year's salary and, in effect, told to go away and stay away. He might be a military hero with the DSO and the American Legion of Merit but it was clear that Enid's future was more important to Newnes than his. She had made her feelings plain. A less sensitive and decent man might have threatened to sue and provide both the publishers and Enid with some unpleasant publicity. As it was, Hugh received an official invitation from the War Office to write the history of the Normandy invasion, which occupied his time and his talents for the next five years.

As a child, Enid Blyton used to tell herself stories in bed before going to sleep. Often enough, in these stories she was the heroine. If this kind of day-dreaming is indulged strongly over the years, the subject may harbour a tendency to believe that he or she is always in the right and other people wrong; that those who run counter to his or her wishes are bad and dangerous; that they must be punished, taught the error of their ways. This is one possible, if rather crude, explanation of Enid's behaviour towards her first husband, who, it seems, never did her the slightest harm.

The same vindictive streak kept her away for almost thirty years from her mother, who died in the mid-1950s after a long degenerative illness. A bitter row had precipitated the break but Enid would not go to see her, even when she was close to death. She, too, had become an 'un-person', as if in Stalin's Russia, and Kenneth was kept well away from his mother-in-law. Gillian and Imogen never even knew of their grandmother's existence until after her death.

But when the 'romancing' begins to fail, a dormant conscience may be awoken. In August 1957, when Gillian married Donald Baverstock, the brilliant young BBC producer, Enid asked me to stay near the back of St James's Church, Piccadilly, in case Hugh made a sudden entrance and 'caused a scene', which was the last thing he would have done.

Green Hedges in Penn Road, Beaconsfield, Enid's home for the last thirty years of her life, was a large detached Edwardian 'stockbroker's Tudor' house, standing some 30 yards back from the road in 2½ acres of garden. On the north side, there were outhouses, occupied by the Rolls Royce, the Bentley and the MG sports car. The house was furnished comfortably but not in great style. A thick high hedge virtually concealed it from passers-by; there were two openings in the hedge connected by a semi-circular gravel drive. In the borders alongside the front of the house there stood small images of Noddy and Big Ears.

In 1950, Enid's writing affairs had been consolidated into a company, Darrell Waters Limited. But Kenneth was about as fitted to run a company of some intricacy as the average accountant would be to perform a heart transplant, and suffered from the extra disability of profound deafness. Also, his deafness made it impossible to carry out a telephone conversation of any length with him. He wore a hearing aid, which crackled and whined in a sinister manner. He never understood that in business giving a little can sometimes lead to gaining a lot. He was justifiably proud of his wife's fame and talent and he wanted to drive the hardest possible bargain on her behalf, apparently unconscious that she was already at the top of the tree. He looked on publishers, stage producers and television operatives as little short of crooks, scheming to plunder his wife's earnings. He should have looked closer to home for crookedness, as a later chapter shows. He even threatened to sue the BBC for libel when one of the characters in the humorous radio series *Take It From Here* said that her little boy was never happier than when 'curled up in front of the fire with Enid Blyton'.

A pleasant little ceremony always took place on the last day of each *Noddy in Toyland* pantomime season. Bertie Meyer and the cast invited Enid and Kenneth to a party. After soft drinks and ice cream for the young cast and somewhat stronger beverages for the adults, a ceremonial cake was cut, speeches were made and everyone dispersed with good cheer and hopes that next year's performances would be equally successful. In 1960, the pantomime was performed at the Scala Theatre and Bertie Meyer booked assembly rooms in nearby Tottenham Court Road for the reception. For some reason, Kenneth did not attend the final performance and Enid was on her own. She had to wait about half an hour after the last curtain, while the cast wiped off their greasepaint and changed into everyday clothes. Her chauffeur had driven her to London in the Rolls Royce and she told me she would be perfectly happy just sitting and resting quietly in the back of the well-upholstered car.

The party was due to begin at 6 o'clock. By quarter past, there was no sign of Enid, usually the most punctual of women. No one wanted to start enjoying the food and drink before the *fons et origo* of their success put in an appearance (the pantomime had been a sell-out for every performance). By 6.30 p.m., the party-goers were all getting worried and I decided to telephone Green Hedges in case there were any messages. To my great surprise, Enid herself answered. She was friendly, as always, but clearly surprised by my call.

It was the first recorded instance of the onset of Alzheimer's disease, which was to kill her in another eight sad years. In those days, it would have taken about three-quarters of an hour to drive to Beaconsfield from central London and so she must have told the chauffeur to take her home within minutes of my bidding her a temporary *au revoir* outside the theatre.

As the years went by, she had her lucid moments when one could almost imagine that the old Enid Blyton was back with us in all her mental alertness. But gradually those moments became fewer and fewer. She would type out old published stories and, later, confusing them with original scripts, send them on to me to place with a publisher, which with some subterfuge or other I never did. Kenneth spun a protective cocoon around her, too protective, perhaps, for he destroyed all but one of the diaries she had kept since 1937 (an invaluable source for a biographer or critic), but he too was becoming a very sick man. The arthritis in his neck and hips had grown worse and was extremely painful. He overdosed himself with supposedly curative drugs and increasing amounts of painkillers. He eventually died in September 1967 and Enid survived him by fourteen months, dying in a nursing home in Hampstead on 28 November 1968.

In her lonely year at Green Hedges, virtually none of her many publishers took the time and the trouble to call on her. Why pursue the golden goose when it has stopped laying and one already possesses several of its golden eggs? However, they all flocked to her memorial service at St James's Church, Piccadilly, a far more convenient meeting place, in January 1969. In his address, Paul Hodder-Williams, chairman of Hodder & Stoughton, said 'She really loved children and understood instinctively what would interest them'.

Perhaps the final word should go to the psychologist, Michael Woods, who wrote, 'She was a child, she thought as a child and she wrote as a child . . .' (*Blyton Revisited*, a special edition of *LINES*, Autumn 1969).

STYLE AND CONTENT

Evelyn Waugh wrote an interesting article in the *Cornhill Magazine* not long after the war in which he equated contemporary prose styles with the writing implements available at the time. Thus, the eighteenth-century quill pen, which required frequent pauses for re-sharpening, gave rise to the balanced, antithetical sentences of Augustan prose. The growing use of the fountain pen in late Victorian and Edwardian times made for more flowing and lengthy paragraphs, while the typewriter in the 1920s helped to develop a staccato style and the dictating machine, which was coming into vogue when he wrote and which was his bane, gave rise to prolix verbiage. He did not live long enough to encounter the impersonality of the word processor.

Enid Blyton was a typewriter devotee. Her ancient manual machine still occupies a place of honour at the Enid Blyton Company's offices. Her methods were quite extraordinary. On the south side of Green Hedges there was a veranda or lean-to with sufficient space for two or three chairs. After breakfast most mornings, Enid would wrap a shawl round her shoulders and sit on a hard chair with a plank across her knees and the portable typewriter balanced on the plank. She would, she once told me, try to clear her mind of all other details and concentrate on the work in hand. She needed to come up with a short strong action sentence to open with. Once found, it unlocked her sub-conscious mind. The words flowed as fast as she could get them on to paper – and she became an expert typist. When the text was finished, she would have it professionally retyped before handing it to a publisher, but, as her agent, I saw many of her drafts, when completed, and apart from a rare crossing-out, they were word-perfect and could have gone straight into production.

Her powers of concentration and her durability were, in my fairly wide experience of authors at work, unique. On one occasion, I had assembled several queries and small problems which required decisions from her and I telephoned to suggest calling in at Green Hedges one afternoon in the coming week to sort them out over a cup of tea. When assured that none of them was very urgent, she asked if my visit could be postponed until the following week. 'You see, George,' she said, 'I have to deliver the new Famous Five, as you know, by the end of next week – and I haven't started it yet. I've promised Kenneth to play golf with him on Friday afternoon, so I'll have my work cut out to finish it by then.'

Flaubert might spend a whole morning deciding whether to put a comma in or take it out. He was an extreme case, but many serious novelists would consider it a good morning's work if they put 200 publishable words on to paper. To average 1,000 words per day in a five-day working week would mean finishing a full-length novel in under six months. Most authors usually take a good deal longer than that.

A Famous Five novel runs to between 40,000 and 50,000 words in length. To write one in four-and-a-half days means a daily average of about 10,000 words. Allowing perhaps seven hours' writing (or typing) in two morning and afternoon stints means producing an average of 1,500 words an hour. It is an amazing record. She did, in fact, finish the story by lunch time that Friday and enjoyed her golfing break with Kenneth in the afternoon.

Early in 1953, a young psychologist named Peter McKellar, who was carrying out research for a thesis at Aberdeen University, wrote to her, asking for insights into a writer's imagery processes. Her reply ran to more than a thousand words; she was clearly touched by his interest. Here are some extracts from her letter, which differ in some degree from what she had said to me:

> In my case, the imagery began as a young child. In bed I used to shut my eyes and 'let my mind go free'. And into it would come what I call my 'night stories' – which were, in effect, all kinds of imaginings in story form – sometimes I was the 'I' in the story, sometimes I wasn't. . . .
>
> . . . Because of this imagining I wanted to write – to put down what I had seen and felt and heard in my imagination. I had a gift for words, so it was easy. . . .
>
> . . . First of all, you must realise that when I begin a completely new book with new characters, I have no idea at all what the characters will be, where the story will happen, or what adventures or events will

occur. All I know is that the book is to be, say, an 'Adventure' tale or a 'Mystery' or a 'fairy-tale' and so on, that it must be a certain length – say, 40,000 words.

I shut my eyes for a few minutes, with my portable typewriter on my knee – I make my mind a blank and wait – and then, as clearly as I would see real children, my characters stand before me in my mind's eye. I see them in detail – hair, eyes, feet, clothes, expression – and I always know their Christian names but never their surname. (I get these out of a telephone directory afterwards!) . . . As I look at them, the characters take on movement and life – they talk and laugh (I hear them) and perhaps I see that one of them has a dog, or a parrot, and I think – 'Ah – that's good. That will liven up the story.'

. . . That's enough for me. My hands go down on my typewriter keys and I begin. . . . The story is enacted in my mind's eye almost as if I had a private cinema there. The characters come on and off, talk, laugh, sing – have their adventures – quarrel – and so on. I watch and hear everything, writing it down with my typewriter. . . . I don't know what anyone is going to say or do. I don't know what is going to happen. I am in the happy position of being able to write a story and read it for the first time, at one and the same moment.

. . . Another odd thing is that my 'under-mind'
seems to be able to receive such directions as 'the
story must be 40,000 words long'. Because, sure
enough, no matter what length I have to write to (it
varies tremendously) the book ends almost to the
word – the right length.

When news of her unusual methods of
composition emerged, several critics and journalists
poured scorn on them. 'Writing in a trance' was a
headline and one of the more literate opponents
closed his sarcastic diatribe by translating the Latin
tag: '*Finis coronat opus*' – 'The end justifies the
means'. Enid Blyton could have retorted with
Sir Christopher Wren's epigram: '*Si monumentum
requiris, circumspice*' – 'If you seek my memorial, look
around you'. Every bookshop and library would
have dozens of her books on their shelves.

Nevertheless, she gave hostages to fortune by
writing to all the leading literary editors, asking
them not to review her books but to give the space
thus made available to less well-known writers. She
told so many of her friends about this generous
gesture that in the end she must have convinced
herself that it was indeed so. She had wiped from
her mind the double suspicion that literary editors

might not consider her books worth reviewing or, if they did find room, the resulting reviews might be caustically adverse. In any case, her books sold in copious quantities without the benefit of reviews.

Apart from possessing the ability to tap her subconscious so positively, Enid Blyton was a true professional in technique and speed of thought. I was witness to this on one occasion when rehearsals were under way for the first ever performance of the *Noddy in Toyland* pantomime. Well into the plot, Enid had introduced the Saucepan Man, who was to become quite a major character. In the original version, he just walked on and said who he was. Bertie Meyer, the producer, and André van Gyseghen, the director, both felt he needed a more memorable entrance – a musical one. Enid and I called on Philip Green, the composer of much of the *Noddy* music, at his Regent's Park flat. He had already been warned on the telephone of the problem and was soon sitting at his grand piano, strumming and striking chords until they coalesced into a jaunty rhythm, which went 'dee-dum, dum, dum, dee-dum, dum, dum, dum, dum, dum, deedle-deedle, dum.' 'Come on, Enid,' Phil said. 'All we want now is the words.'

She asked him to play the little tune over again, which he did, and then with hardly a pause, she came out with:

I'm the Saucepan Man, the Saucepan Man,
I'll sell you a kettle or a pan,
Or a nice little watering can,
Because – I am – the Saucepan Man.

It was not great poetry but it was just what was needed – a satisfying impromptu that brought an important character into play with a flourish.

During and since her lifetime, Enid Blyton has been accused of racism, chauvinism, anti-feminism, caste-consciousness and all the other sins in the *fin de siècle* libertarian calendar. She was accused of introducing black golliwogs as the naughty characters in some of her fairy stories. However, the accusers conveniently forgot that for generations small children had been enchanted with the black golliwog featured on the labels of Robertson's jam and marmalade. She was criticized because any foreigners cropping up in her books for older children were seen either as figures of fun or villains. The secret gangs who carried out the various adventures were dominated by boys and tomboyish girls, such as Georgina the Famous Five character, who was always known as 'George'. There were gardeners and cooks among the minor characters but they knew their place and metaphorically touched their forelocks when the young master or mistress passed. Even the police showed 'proper' respect for the upper middle classes.

Anyone born and reared since 1960 must find it difficult, almost impossible, to understand and appreciate the Edwardian era in which Enid Blyton grew up and which coloured her conscious and subconscious thought. In 1911, the new king, George V, attended the magnificent Durbar in Delhi, where the Indian princes and maharajahs prostrated themselves before his throne. For he was the King Emperor, the 'master of the world', over a fifth of which, the British Empire, he ruled. Few people alive then, apart perhaps from Herr Spengler, realized that this was the British Empire's peak and that from then on it would be all downhill. Even the tragic loss of so many fine young men killed in action in the First World War failed to lower the confidence that 'Britons never shall be slaves' and that on the far side of the Channel there were 'lesser breeds without the law'.

In 1971, Colin Watson published a witty and trenchant book entitled *Snobbery with Violence*. It dealt with crime writers of thirty or forty years earlier and demonstrated the unconscious racism, anti-semitism and over-emphasis on class that affected authors like Edgar Wallace, 'Sapper', Leslie Charteris and Dorothy L. Sayers. These were only typical of many more – Agatha Christie wrote a detective novel, later adapted as a stage play, entitled *Ten Little Niggers*, the opening words of a popular contemporary rhyme. In the 1930s, clothes shops sold skirts and stockings in a shade known as 'nigger brown'.

Enid Blyton was a child of her times. She grew up in a much stricter age when the attitude was commonly:

> God bless the squire and his relations
> And keep us in our proper stations.

People advanced as far as talent and hard work could take them but did not ape the gentry.

To apply the strict rules of literary criticism to Enid Blyton's writing would be both unfair and absurd. Her forte was telling stories and her technique was adapted for that purpose. Her sentences tend to be simple and straightforward, with very few dependent clauses. There are few adjectives and those used are the more obvious ones – 'a hot sunny day', 'a short nap', 'sharp eyes', 'poor Margery' and so on. Much of the story development takes place through dialogue, which contains a liberal peppering of exclamation marks. The opening paragraph of *Last Term at Malory Towers* (1951) is typical:

'My last term!' thought Darrell, as she got ready to go downstairs. 'My very last term! I shall be eighteen on my next birthday – I'm almost grown-up!'

For a young reader coming fresh to the Malory Towers series, those three simple sentences could make an irresistible lead-in. The strangely named girl is going back to school for the last time, she must be one of the senior girls judging by her age and, somehow, the exclamation marks imply that there are exciting times ahead. When a keen reader critic asked Nevil Shute, another great storyteller, what was the secret of his technique, he answered, 'Simple. When readers get to the bottom of a righthand page, I want them to turn over and see what happens on the next lefthand page.' Enid Blyton could have given the same answer.

Malory Towers ran to six titles, as did her other school series, St Clare's. Both of these series were centred around boarding schools. She had been quick to realize the drama inherent in a closed society, as indeed in the adult market at about the same time had C.P. Snow in his novels about struggles for power inside a Cambridge college. Enid had an added advantage in that her daughters were boarders at Benenden School, and she would be able to consult them about modern customs at school, what kind of practical jokes were played on the mistresses and crushes and cliques. Perhaps a clue to the invisible aid afforded most probably by Gillian can be seen in the heroine of *Last Term at Malory Towers*, Darrell Rivers (as opposed to 'Waters'). And one paragraph must have touched stepfather Kenneth's heart:

Darrell stood up suddenly. She felt really sick. She thought of her own father, Mr Rivers — kindly, hard-working surgeon, devoted to his wife and two daughters. How would he feel if she, Darrell, suddenly 'stood up' to him, and spoke cruel words, as Gwen had to her father?

It almost appears that Enid Blyton in her stream of consciousness approach to creative writing had obliterated the real father of her children, Hugh Pollock, from her subconscious mind and had substituted Kenneth, the 'hard-working surgeon'.

Not for nothing had Enid been a Sunday school teacher in her younger days. There is a high moral purpose in much of the action she describes. In one of the Malory Towers books, Amanda Chartelow, an older girl, has come to the school because her previous school was burned down during the holidays. She is an excellent swimmer, almost of Olympic standard, but is headstrong and vain. She claims to need a big area of water in which to train to the best advantage, but the headmistress warns her against swimming in the nearby sea because of its dangerous currents. Amanda disobeys her, swims out to sea, gets caught up in the treacherous crossflow and, exhausted, is being swept out to sea when June, the girl she had bullied throughout the term, comes out in a rowing boat and rescues her. Again, Gwen, the daughter of a rich father, is stuck-up and rude to all her classmates. But her father falls seriously ill, and instead of going to a finishing school in Switzerland, she has to leave Malory Towers and take a job. Chastened, she writes a letter, apologizing for all her rudeness and hoping her classmates will keep in touch. The next paragraph reads:

> Darrell did write, of course. She wrote at once. Darrell was happy and had a happy future to look forward to, and she could well afford to spill a little happiness into Gwen's dull and humdrum life.

An older reader might hope fervently that happy Darrell would fall under the next bus that came along for being so smug and patronizing, but young readers presumably swallow the sugar-coated pill.

Morality is sometimes handled rather more subtly, as in *Those Dreadful Children*. The rather prim and proper John and his two sisters, Margery and Annette, discover that the Taggerty children have moved in next door. The Taggertys, Pat, Maureen and Biddy, are rough-and-tumble little rapscallions with their dog Dopey. There are various adventures, including quarrels and some horse-play, until finally the prim children come to enjoy the easygoing attitudes of the ones who have become their new friends, while the newcomers have lost the selfishness and pugnacity they brought with them.

One is virtually certain to reach a happy ending in an Enid Blyton story. *The Family at Red-Roofs* is typical. Mr and Mrs Jackson have four children, the eldest of whom is Molly, sixteen, followed by Peter, fourteen. The family moves into its new home, which is larger and roomier than anything they have lived in before. Molly is due to leave school at the end of the summer term, but she has already been invited to become a trainee teacher in the kindergarten of her school and learn Froebel methods – another autobiographical touch on the part of the author. Peter wants to pass his exams and study to become a doctor. There is the usual arrogant and unpleasant rich girl at the school – Prudence, who upsets all her acquaintances.

Mr Jackson's firm sends him to the USA for six months on business. During the outward voyage, the liner is in a collision and he is reported missing, believed drowned. The family has almost no capital and the elder children give up their ambitions. As the book was published before the Welfare State was in place, one might have expected Mr Jackson's employers to treat the bereaved family with some generosity – which they do not – since the father was only carrying out their orders. Molly becomes a nursemaid in a dirty and unpleasant household and Peter an office boy in a publishing house. Even the younger children help, the small boy mending watches and clocks – he has a mechanical bent – and his sister fetching the damaged ones and returning the repaired items in her doll's pram.

Then – hooray! – Mr Jackson is found to be alive in the USA. He had been rescued from the sea but was suffering from amnesia after a blow to his head. He is flown home amid great newspaper publicity. Meanwhile, Prudence's father has lost all his money with the collapse of his business and, having flaunted her wealth and possessions for over three-quarters of the text, she has to beg forgiveness and seek a small furnished room in the Jackson house. The older reader can almost hear the Sunday school teacher's tones – the proud shall be brought down, the meek shall inherit the earth, do as you would be done by – in this and many other of Enid Blyton's texts. It is ironic that one of the two richest women writers then alive, the other being Agatha Christie, should extol the merits of poverty and hard work. But Enid Blyton was no hypocrite. For creative purposes her emotions were still centred on the little girl of thirteen whose father had gone away and who had to work all the harder at school to prove herself and had learned to cope with questions, whether innocent or barbed, from her school mates about his absence. She believed sincerely that determination and hard work would always win the day, as evidenced by her own spectacular financial success.

Conversely, when compared with the whimsical humour of A.A. Milne, the realistic humour of Richmal Crompton and the sardonic humour of Roald Dahl, all of whom were Enid Blyton's contemporaries, her efforts at humour do not shine. Typical, perhaps, is the incident in *Last Term at Malory Towers*, where a tomboy takes a powerful magnet into class when Mam'zelle Dupont, the French mistress, is teaching. Mam'zelle has long hair pinned up with metal hairpins. The girl goes up to her desk, manages to stand behind her and holds the magnet close to the back of her head. The pins fly out on to the magnet and the teacher's hair comes tumbling down, much to her surprise and annoyance. It was clearly a favourite practical joke for the author, who had used exactly the same method with another Mam'zelle, the French teacher in *Fifth Form at St Clare's*, published six years earlier.

In the forty years since Enid Blyton was at the zenith of her powers, moral and educational standards have changed. Novels for teenagers nowadays are often far more 'grown up' in their approach, conveying openly a limited amount of sexual attraction through their themes. However, there is clearly a very solid market for the old-fashioned virtues of an Enid Blyton story. Her characters, even the sixteen- and seventeen-year-old schoolgirls, seem to be crystallized into a pre-sex state. There are no flirtations with boys, no talk even of boyfriends. The stories could in fact be played out in a convent. This would be normal enough for the early readers of Enid Blyton, most of whom were girls (they are still by a large majority her main readers). But there must be something special about the books to keep a far more sophisticated readership contented and asking for more in the present age.

Can that special quality be defined? An important part of it is what politicians have recently come to describe as 'the feelgood factor'. There is always a happy ending. Goodness is rewarded and naughtiness punished. The characters have learned through their experiences and even the conceited ones who have been abased have resolved to be and do better in future. In the words of Miss Theobald, the head mistress at Malory Towers, 'Those girls who faced their difficulties, saw and understood their faults, conquered their failings, and became strong characters and leaders would make the finest wives and mothers of the future.' It is an orderly world with rules and regulations which, once understood and accepted, provide a comfortable – and comforting – background.

These qualities, however admirable on their own, will not make a book popular. It could well end up as a dry-as-dust moral tome. Enid Blyton had an extra secret, probably an unconscious one. Galileo uttered it, when tortured on the rack: *'Eppur se muove'* – 'And yet it moves'. Raymond Chandler had the same idea in a very different context when he said, 'When in doubt, bring in a man with a gun in his hand'. Above all, keep it moving. Enid Blyton did that superbly well from her days as a Sunday school teacher to the end of her long career. Grab their attention right away and hold it through action and more action. She set a scene quickly and then with her short paragraphs and stripped-down sentences kept the characters on the move. There were no pauses for detailed descriptions of the scenery or subtle characterization. Young readers had to use their imaginations to fill in the gaps, a better mental exercise, it might be claimed, than watching explicit television images.

And, finally, there is something comforting about the familiar. If a young reader has read and enjoyed a couple of Famous Five books, the fact that there are seventeen others ready and waiting – if pocket money permits – is reassuring. Most of the other series have fewer titles, but together they provide a warm blanket for the early teenage reader. There is a solidity about the Enid Blyton fictional world that young people in our insecure age must find appealing. The sun shines continually, families stick together, there is no real cruelty or savage behaviour, crimes are either petty or smartly suppressed by the forces of law, aided, of course, by the boy and girl characters.

In the 1970s, many libraries and bookshops refused to stock Enid Blyton titles. However, the National Centre for Research into Children's Literature has now stamped her books with its seal of approval. At its spring conference in 1997, Anne Fine, a noted children's author and Carnegie Medal winner, said, 'Enid Blyton should be saluted for her contribution to children's literacy by hooking millions of us on reading. . . . She knew what we were dreaming about. You wanted to be in her free, airy world of caves and coves and secret tunnels and, most importantly, absentee parents.'

Professor Fred Inglis said, 'We have become too tied up over whether Blyton is racist or sexist. Books should make you happy. I remember Enid Blyton making me happy and we must hang on to that.' Nicholas Tucker, a child psychology lecturer at Sussex University, said that the unrealistic plots are heroic daydreams that children find flattering.

But the professor and the lecturer are clever men, approaching a vast subject from a specialized angle. To Enid, it was a much simpler formula, which could be expressed in four words, 'Tell me a story'. It is an age-old plea, from the mouths of the young and from adult readers of novels and viewers of the cinema and television screens. With her talents honed as a teacher by years of telling stories to her pupils and then trying out her written tales on them and, later, encouraging her readers to write to her with their comments and, above all, continual practice, she became a storyteller *par excellence*.

DARRELL WATERS LIMITED

A popular author's sales often depend on their originator's ability to stay alive. A living author can attend signing sessions, appear on television and radio programmes and be generally in the news. Each new book published tends to rally the sales of the previous books. After his or her death, the graph may remain steady for a year or two but will then decline into small sales and after an interval no sales at all. Edgar Wallace, 'Sapper' and, in more recent times, Peter Cheyney and John Creasey, in their prime all immensely successful bestsellers, are hardly in print at all these days. Arthur Koestler, who wrote one of the great twentieth-century novels, *Darkness at Noon*, uttered a plea that they might all have echoed when he said he would give up a hundred readers now for ten readers in ten years' time and one reader a hundred years from now.

By the same token, Talbot Baines Reid and Angela Brazil, once the most widely read authors of boys' and girls' school stories, are now only footnotes in academic theses. The 'quality' children's writers since the 1920s, Arthur Ransome, A.A. Milne, Richmal Crompton, E. Nesbit and, more recently, Roald Dahl, are still flourishing – and, along with them, Enid Blyton.

Most authors, in particular those who write for children, tend to specialize by writing, for example, only adventure stories or school stories or science fiction. In addition, they also tend to concentrate on a fairly narrow range of ages. Whether by accident or shrewd design, Enid Blyton wrote all manner of stories for all age groups from four to fourteen. She also took early advantage of the spread of paperback editions. The result was that, without any proper guidance from an expert in the book trade, from her death until the fairly recent sale of the company, her books averaged annual sales of 3 or 4 million copies within the United Kingdom and 5 to 6 million copies in the rest of the world (including sales in translation).

The continuing sales in such vast quantities constituted a fitting memorial for a writer who could touch her young readers' hearts. They also gave rich pickings for a predator.

Eric Rogers had been the jolly eminence behind Darrell Waters Limited ever since its formation in 1950. As a result, the deaths of Kenneth in 1967 and of Enid the following year made little difference to the running of the company. Eric was short, rosy-cheeked, with twinkling eyes and a cherubic smile. He was quick of speech and quick of wit. The senior partner in a small stockbroking firm, he had acted for Wilfred Harvey, the unscrupulous printing entrepreneur, and had been introduced to the Darrell Waters by one of Harvey's directors.

To the basically simple-minded Kenneth, who had spent his life in medical circles, Eric Rogers was the acme of City sophistication. The pair also shared a keen interest in horse-racing, fine wines, Havana cigars – and money. There is no doubt that, in the early days, Eric did make money for Kenneth and Enid from shrewd investments on the Stock Exchange. He was also, it appears, feathering his own nest by running an expensive Bentley at least partly on the company and lunching most weekdays at his corner table in the Savoy Restaurant, again courtesy of DWL.

He came into his own after the organization's two founding members had died. He was then well into his seventies. He was grooming his daughter Patricia, who had become a director on Enid's death, to succeed him as chairman and thus keep the company 'in the family', but she was tragically killed in a Turkish Airlines crash in the early 1970s. He then appointed a junior executive from his City office to join the board. Gillian and Imogen, who were also directors, were both married with growing families and had their own interests – in Gillian's case, following her mother as a school teacher. They attended board meetings, but left the day-to-day running of the company, naturally enough, to the man who had long possessed Enid's and Kenneth's trust.

Eric Rogers's first significant step was to have Green Hedges, its outhouses and the carefully nurtured fruit and vegetable garden demolished and the resulting acreage sold for development. Had it been put to them, Enid's major publishers would almost certainly have helped to fund Green Hedges as a permanent Blyton memorial-cum-museum with a book and toy shop and open-air play sites for young visitors. Entrance charges and profits from the shop would have covered the running costs. But it was not to be. Eric had no feeling for what Enid's fans might want, preferring to concentrate on making a quick profit with as little difficulty as possible. He had written himself into the wills of Enid and Kenneth, with the result that, as beneficial trustee for the bulk of their shares, he controlled the company and could do whatever he wanted.

One example of his autonomy was when he borrowed £150,000 (worth about £600,000 in today's terms) from the company. Clearly, he never intended to repay the loan, which was still outstanding at his death in 1980 and which had to be written off. For a rich man to borrow money that he does not need from the company of his late friends with no intention of repaying the loan, secure in the knowledge that the transaction will only be revealed after his death, constitutes a particularly shabby form of fraud.

Once Enid stopped writing, Darrell Waters Limited had really become a one-author literary agency, handling the rights worldwide for over six hundred titles. Translating the figures into present-day values, the turnover in 1970 was about £500,000, in 1975 about £875,000 and in 1980 —

an exceptional year – upwards of £1.5 million. The overheads in later years amounted to over 40 per cent of turnover. Apart from the directors' fees, there were the rent of an office in central London, salaries and wages for staff, company cars, insurance, lighting, heating and telephone bills. With company taxation in the decade after 1968 ranging as high as 52 per cent, there was no great incentive to increase profits, but if Eric had wanted to build up the value of the estate for the family's benefit, he could have invited one of the larger agencies to use its expert knowledge of rights' markets to enhance turnover at a maximum charge of 10 per cent. There would then have been no need for an expensive additional office or staff salaries. The agency would cover such costs out of its commission. But that move would have prevented Eric from keeping more than one finger in the pie; he never explored it.

In 1968, the British Copyright Act protected the rights up to the end of the fiftieth year after the author's death. In other words, after 31 December 2018, all the Blyton titles would automatically go out of copyright. It made no difference that they had been assigned to a company that was still in existence. In 1995, in order to fall into line with other countries in the European Union, British copyright protection was increased to a period of seventy years after death. By then, over half the original period of protection had lapsed but now the 'unexpired portion' of twenty-three years had been almost doubled. The overall value of such a steady and substantial earner, year in, year out, increased enormously.

Eric Rogers's nominee, Margaret Eve, resigned her directorship in the mid-1980s. From that time, the family tried with varying success to run the company, aided for a brief period by Alasdair Milne, lately Director-General of the BBC, and for an even briefer period by myself. Gillian was a busy and successful school teacher in Yorkshire, whose husband Donald was in poor health and thus in need of frequent attention. She was unable to spend much time in London, except during the school holidays. Imogen had little business experience, but had firm convictions about what ought to be done. Both of them were – indeed, are – women of strong opinions and there were inevitably arguments and mis-understandings. I was sometimes reminded of the old army saying, 'Order, counter-order – disorder'.

After several years of internal strife, the eventual solution was to find a buyer for the company, with the proviso that either Gillian or Imogen remained as an active director to ensure that the spirit of their mother's books remained intact and that the texts were left basically in their pristine condition. There had been some tactful bowdlerizing in recent years, in which the black golliwogs had vanished. Some of the illustrations had also been modernized, but on the whole nothing had been done which might have upset an original fan.

The Blyton stories had never been hugely successful in the USA. About forty years earlier, a small publishing house in Chicago had issued a few Famous Five titles with a conspicuous lack of success. In the late 1980s, strenuous efforts were made to launch a range of books there and the head of one new paperback house was on the point of making a commitment when problems arose with his backers. Historically, the tastes of American and British adult readers tend to converge, with the Britons rather more prepared to read about and understand American mores than vice versa. But, for whatever reason, there is a wide divergence between popular reading for American children and their British counterparts. Since Louisa M. Alcott's day, there has hardly been a single American children's novel which has found favour on this side of the Atlantic and, with the exception of a few 'quality' authors like A.A. Milne, the same fate has awaited popular British writers for juveniles in the USA.

There is no exact method for calculating the value of a literary agency. Most of them, being privately owned and controlled by their respective boards of directors, tend to avoid paying more tax than absolutely necessary by increasing legitimate expenses like salaries and overseas travel. An investor, knowing that a bank would pay up to 7 per cent interest, should expect a return of at least 12½ per cent on a more risky venture. Few could be considered riskier than an agency depending on one dead author who might slip out of fashion.

The company's pre-tax profits for the last three years of its private ownership averaged out at about £558,400. On a factor of 8 (i.e. 12½ per cent return on capital outlay), Darrell Waters Limited would have an approximate valuation of £4.5 million. There was almost £1.5 million of retained profits in the business, which would increase the valuation to

£6 million. Overheads were exceptionally high at an annual average of nearly £400,000 and absorption into a much larger and well-run organization might save perhaps £250,000 a year in that area – £2 million on an eight-year run. These various factors would make the overall value about £8 million. When Trocadero PLC purchased the company in February 1995, at once renaming it what it should always have been called – the Enid Blyton Company – the purchase price was announced as £14.6 million.

These calculations are rough and ready and made without access to the company's inner records. There may be nuggets hidden away from the outside observer. But at first sight it appears that the price paid was overly generous – unless, that is, the new management is able to exploit the American market. If this is achieved, it may seem the smartest move since Manhattan was bought from the Mohican tribe for a string of beads. Almost immediately, in March 1997, Trocadero announced plans for launching a series of Noddy television films on the American market. If that enterprise were to succeed, it would establish a beach head not only for the Noddy books but also for other series by Enid Blyton.

But the going could be tough. One of the advantages of longevity in the children's book world is that the new generation of mothers recalls with affection the stories they grew up with and are likely to encourage *their* children to read those very same stories. For example, a woman born in 1920 might at the age of ten have enjoyed *Sunny Stories*. She might well pass her taste for Enid Blyton on to her own daughter, born in the mid-1940s. That daughter could have had children of her own in the 1970s, who were steered towards the Blyton books, and by the 1990s a fourth generation has begun to grow up. In other words, a ready-made market has existed for well over sixty years. But this applies only to Great Britain, various Commonwealth countries and perhaps one or two Scandinavian countries where English has long been the second language. The USA market, the biggest and thus the most important book market in the world, comes cold to the concept of Enid Blyton and, therefore, the launching struggle is all the more difficult.

With or without the USA, Enid Blyton has still been an outstanding publishing phenomenon. In the crudest terms, for a literary estate to be worth many millions of pounds thirty years after the author's death is an extraordinary and unmatched situation. Without special publicity, the vast array of titles has sold a total of 10 million copies, year in, year out, ever since her death – an average of over 15,000 copies for each individual title right across the board. Today, an adult novel that sold 15,000 copies would automatically be on the bestseller list and a publisher might consider a firm sale of 3,000 copies of a new book for children more than adequate. In view of these statistics, the sales appeal of Enid Blyton stands out in more than stark contrast.

For touching children's hearts and then holding their interest, generation after generation, in spite of the conflicting attractions first of the radio and then of television, Enid Blyton was truly unique.

CONCLUSION

Not long after Enid Blyton's death, a letter appeared in the *Bookseller*, proposing that the book trade should club together and erect a statue to her, celebrating her devoted service to their cause over many years. The letter was not entirely tongue in cheek, although, as was only to be expected, booksellers did not rush forward to fund the good cause. But they did undeniably benefit from the collective millions of her books they had sold over the years and were continuing to sell after her death.

Children, who have been encouraged to read by Blyton from the age of three until reaching puberty, grow into adults. Accustomed to picking up a book and reading it, they may well continue with the habit in spite of the growing counterclaims of mobile telephones, digital television, virtual reality and the internet. The adult readers will, of course, move on to more sophisticated stories, but in quite a few cases it will have been Enid Blyton who started them on the path of reading for pleasure.

There has been an interesting change of climate in the past thirty or forty years. In the 1950s and '60s, school teachers wrote letters to the press condemning the Blyton books for being old fashioned, snobbish, racist and written in pre-digested prose. Some public librarians went so far as to ban the books from their shelves. Those teachers and librarians acted from the standpoint of a thorough grounding in the 'Three Rs'. Now teachers and librarians are coming round to the idea that Enid Blyton wrote clear, grammatical prose and that, as a former teacher herself who was kept up to date by innumerable letters and cards from her young readers, she knew the appeal of a fast-moving, eventful story. They are beginning to recommend her as an author who will encourage pupils to read – and go on reading.

If each of the 600-plus books Enid Blyton wrote over forty years averaged 15,000 words in length, that would amount to 9 million words or, allowing for her annual holiday at Swanage in the second half of the period, just over 1,000 words a day every weekday throughout all those years. Most successful professional novelists would reckon it a very good day when they produced 500 words, a rate at which they could complete a full-length novel in under a year. And then they would spend the next six months resting, proof correcting, undertaking publicity appearances and even thinking about a new subject. But Blyton was a unique phenomenon in the publishing world. True, George Simenon wrote 500 novels under various names and John Creasey brought out 560, again using pseudonyms, while Barbara Cartland is closing fast with over 500 books published, including at least five auto-biographies, but she has been writing for seventy years. Nevertheless, Blyton stands out as the most prolific author of the twentieth century. Her world sales total well over 400 million copies – and rising.

Enid Blyton spent so many of her daytime hours locked up in the circle of herself, oblivious to the outside world as she conjured up waking dreams for children of many different races and backgrounds to respond to with delight. Perhaps, as Alzheimer's took its grip, the waking dream became more attractive than reality, cushioned as that was by an attentive husband and plenty of money until in the end it superseded reality.

The last word goes to an old business friend of hers. He wrote:

My abiding memory of Enid Blyton comes from her latter days, on one of the last few times I visited her at Green Hedges. We happened to be standing in the dining room, which doubled as a library. The side walls contained glass-fronted bookcases which held an almost comprehensive sample of her multi-hundred different titles. She was in a lucid period and had been telling me how much she missed Kenneth, and how she would often look up from a newspaper or magazine and quote some interesting point, imagining that he was still sitting in the armchair opposite. To comfort her, I made a fatuous remark about how fortunate she was to have her own children, her two grown-up daughters, each with a family coming along.

'Children?' said Enid. She opened her arms wide, half turning as if to embrace the bookcases on the wall behind. 'These are my children'.

BIBLIOGRAPHY

The place of publication is London unless otherwise stated.

McKellar, Peter. *Imagination and Thinking*, Cohen and West, 1957

Ray, Sheila. *The Blyton Phenomenon*, Andre Deutsch, 1982

Rice, Eva. *Who's Who in Enid Blyton*, Richard Cohen Books, 1997

Stoney, Barbara. *Enid Blyton*, Hodder & Stoughton, 1974 (revised edition, 1992)

Smallwood, Imogen. *A Childhood at Green Hedges*, Methuen, 1989

Summerfield, Tony and Wright, Norman (co-editors). *The Enid Blyton Literary Society Journal* (published twice yearly)

Welch, Colin. 'Dear Little Noddy – A Parent's Lament', *Encounter* (January 1958)

POCKET BIOGRAPHIES

AVAILABLE

Beethoven
Anne Pimlott Baker

Scott of the Antarctic
Michael De-la-Noy

Alexander the Great
E.E. Rice

Sigmund Freud
Stephen Wilson

Marilyn Monroe
Sheridan Morley and
Ruth Leon

Rasputin
Harold Shukman

Jane Austen
Helen Lefroy

Mao Zedong
Delia Davin

Ellen Terry
Moira Shearer

David Livingstone
C.S. Nicholls

Abraham Lincoln
H.G. Pitt

Charles Dickens
Catherine Peters

Marie and Pierre Curie
John Senior

Margot Fonteyn
Alastair Macaulay

Winston Churchill
Robert Blake

Enid Blyton
George Greenfield

FORTHCOMING

George IV
Michael De-la-Noy

Christopher Wren
James Chambers

W.G. Grace
Donald Trelford

Che Guevara
Andrew Sinclair

The Brontës
Kathryn White

Martin Luther King
Henry Harmer

Lawrence of Arabia
Jeremy Wilson

Christopher Columbus
Peter Rivière